Copyright © 2018 by JLS, Inc

All rights reserved. No part of this book may be reproduced in any form whatsoever, without permission in writing from the publisher.

Published by Kind Heart Productions, LLC under license from JLS, Inc

info@kindheartproductions.com

www.kindheartproductions.com

Cover design and Illustrations by

Alexandra Buslova

albus239@gmail.com

ISBN 978-1-7325898-0-3

Happy Landings!

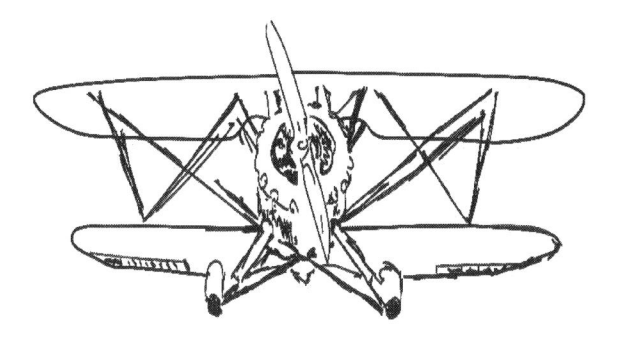

It's true for everyone.

Keep a few pages about the adventures and the ideas that have touched you, hold the pages in a box, add new pages every year, and you'll have a book!

When you do this, you'll have a living record of the events that have changed you from who you were, into who you are today. Every idea needs just a few sentences, a few words and you'll remember those moments, forever.

Perhaps the time will come when your child or your significant other will wish they could have watched, as you grew. Find that box, filled now with pages of the thoughts, of the startlements you've caught on paper before they flew away, and hand it wordlessly, to your friendly inquirer.

I'll guarantee that they will see the person you've yearned to be, the one you've hidden from every stranger who never asked.

You'll also find a day when you'll be free to hand your book to others, as I hand this to you.

Some pages may mirror reflections of the pages of your own life, others may border on the gently bizarre, thoughts you may not have considered before.

I was touched by the thought of my dear friends who said it would be well to print this book, instead of handing you a hundred plus loose pages on a windy day.

With thanks to these remarkable souls, I hand this book to you. I offer my thanks for your curiosity and my wish to survive in your own mind, listening to the ideas that have made a difference for you.

If you enjoy an ancient art, you might notice, too, that when you flip these pages quickly, an image appears that says everything this book means, without a word.

Wishing you joy always,

> Richard Bach
> Fall, 2018

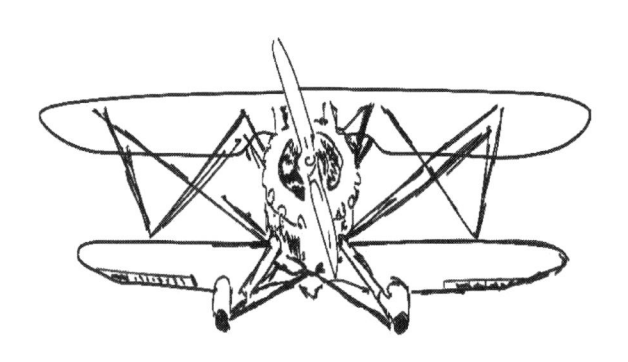

Maxims And Quotes

"*B*efore we can know joy, must we know sorrow." Here's a statement that sounds maxim-pure yet has no truth. "Before we do good, must we do evil?" Sorrow isn't some passive knowledge, sorrow is a feeling we choose to express, actively. These are not sequiturs, there's no sequence there at all. We are every one of us actors -- we can choose any feeling, at any time we wish.

*W*e can count our lives successful when we can touch a tapestry of smiles we've woven.

We have many soulmates. The one who counts is the one with whom we practice our soulmateship.

A book can give viewpoints from within the mind of the writer and within all its characters. No communication has more intimacy than any writer's book.

$\mathcal{A}$ creative, loving-something life, is also a healthy one. There is healing and protection by living what we love.

$\mathcal{A}$ love relationship is like developing a new computer. It begins in a huge mechanical form, needs a large building to keep it from the weather. In time, it streamlines with development and breakthroughs, into microchip simplicity.

Most pilots can remember every flight they've flown.

A hug is an attempt for two to be one. Or it's an attempt by a speaker after a brilliant talk, to hug an entire audience.

$\mathcal{B}$eing concerned about others' lives is like worrying if the pilot of a passing airplane is flying it well. We cannot fly their aircraft, no matter what.

$\mathcal{A}$ person's beauty changes with knowing. Since our consciousness supports our beliefs in appearances, then as we learn some facts about them, their appearance changes, for us.

*A*ll problems have creative solutions, and every problem comes to us with gifts.

I'm not the first to say that selfishness is a lovely thing.

$\mathcal{A}$ place can be beautiful for a homesite, but the belief of an invisible shroud of events, plans, human conditions and attitudes can make it suffocating and unlivable for us.

$\mathcal{D}$on't turn down alternate futures before you're sure you don't even want to taste them. You're always free to change your mind and choose a new future, or a new past, for that matter.

What does this mean? Has it changed our thought? When it hasn't changed our thought, it means nothing.

Anyone, expressing creativity, is beautifully magnetic during their time.

*E*very thought that comes to us is consistent with the others. Each comes with puzzle-hooks, they all connect in some important way. Only if we keep track of the ideas, collect them, will we suddenly see the theme from which our ideas come.

*B*oredom between two people doesn't come from being together physically, but from being separate mentally and spiritually.

Learning one lesson affects every aspect of ourselves.

Each of us is a perfect example of what we believe, a result of a long series of decisions to test ourselves.

Everyone we meet will have a chance for intimacy with us. Most will lose that chance in the first second we meet, as our differences come clear.

If we knew how it was going to turn out, we'd have enjoyed it along the way. We will survive! As soon as we know this, we'll have a perspective that adds so much fun to a lifetime.

*F*un: What was impossible, becomes effortless (reading, learning languages, flying...).

*T*he curse of talent is that we're driven to use it.

$\mathcal{G}$iven the chance, most of us would be brave and glorious human beings. We must find the way to give ourselves that chance.

$\mathcal{H}$appiness is a natural state of consciousness, for all is in a state of well-being. Despair is an altered state based on false appearances and perceptions.

$\mathcal{H}$amlet had no choice whether to be or not to be. BE! is the one command of the universe.

$\mathcal{W}$e test our beliefs by living them.

*O*ur mind is a magnetic experience-organizing field, a network hologram which sorts, sifts, arranges everything it experiences in a certain characteristic way. That unique arrangement may be of interest to others when it is communicated: films, music, books, poems, architecture, dance. When we gain a reputation, we gain it for the mark of that organizing principle that shines through us. Others believe they admire this person. The real admiration is for the magical Arranging Identity that this person represents.

I don't believe in keeping secrets, but neither do I believe in disclosing them to curious others.

Ideas are most easily accepted when they least threaten us.

$\mathcal{R}$emember when we asked where ideas came from, and how rare it was to find a good idea? We grow at different rates into knowing what is a good idea. Our eyes have to adjust to the light and colors, and then we see good ideas everywhere. It is a learning process, and once learned, it is not limited by environment.

$\mathcal{I}$f someone we know can act in this way toward anyone, they can act in this way toward us.

No matter how much we love people, we build walls when too many get close.

Learning, doing something unexpected, ensures we'll be different from day to day.

*L*ove is a harmonic between frequencies. Hate is a perceived discord, unrecognized harmony.

*W*e live like rockets on liftoff: lots of energy and fire and show, yet moving slowly. Later, with much less energy, we're going like crazy.

One reason we have a full life is that we try to anticipate all future problems and plan for them now.

Love stories don't have endings, yet even lovers say, "Good night."

The unseen isn't real, they say. Yet everything we see was once unseen — idea, fantasies, concepts, seeds, images, then objectified for our interest. All comes from and is "what-if" acted out — the virtual in an environment where it's "actual."

The secrets we keep best are the good things we've done. We've been trained to harbor the evil, to remember the bad with guilt, yet there is no corresponding memory-assist for the good things. List the good secrets about ourselves, that we have never shared with others.

They are not sworn secrets, we simply have never chosen to mention them for fear of being thought egocentric. Try listing your divine secrets.

We don't know what's true for us until we're asked to tell somebody else what that may be.

Ideas gather the minds and spirits they need to express themselves in our world.

$\mathcal{T}$he importance of setting a goal is that it pushes us into the river of Process, where we process ourselves, and feel most at home.

$\mathcal{T}$he past gets mashed and compacted in a mental trash-crusher, from which we can recall only pieces that we have to fold flat and smooth to understand.

$\mathcal{A}$re we running away from reality, running away from our time? If this life brings us happiness, if this life is joy for us, then this time is where we belong!

$\mathcal{M}$oney is not the gift we're given. Money is the byproduct of the gifts which we give to others.

We must trust our ideals before we know that they will work. If we did know, there would be no risk, there would be nothing valuable for us to put on line for our beliefs. We mustn't know the reward before we take our risks.

The people in our lives are there as booster rockets. They provide energy and force, but it is we who guide and direct how that force is directed.

$\mathcal{N}$ever take anyone for granted,

whom we prefer to keep in our lives.

$\mathcal{M}$any of our problems begin when

we insulate ourselves from nature.

Our highest self comes to us in ways that we can hear and see and understand.

We're all experienced with lack of success, we know what that is like and what to expect. Success is the unfamiliar, unknown, scary; many blow up at its challenge. When success hits us over the head, it is often with enough force to knock us so far down we never recover, a jump to light-speed that few survive.

$\mathcal{T}$he earth has waited four billion years for us to arrive.

$\mathcal{T}$here must be a two-way empathy in friendships, the circuit must be complete.

*T*o overcome time, love someone and something timeless. This banishes the fear of where we'll be, a hundred years from now.

*W*hat we want is the experience, not the things that bring experience. Not the sailing schooner, but the freedom, the wind, the adventure, the purity of a sailor's life.

$\mathcal{W}$e can tell a lot about a person when we know what gives them comfort.

$\mathcal{T}$hose who allow risks, meet extraordinary people.

We cannot become eternal consumers and remain happy. We must contribute, to give back of what we've learned.

When we write badly, it's nice to know that the best writers write badly too. The difference between the best writers and us, is that they delete all the bad stuff before the book is printed.

$\mathcal{T}$o be "realistic" is to discount our dreams.

$\mathcal{V}$erbalizing sex cheapens it, brings it down. Just experience and grow from it.

𝒯o a writer: What you're doing now is pouring a block of molten words. You'll be shaping it, when it cools, with hammer and chisels, with sandpaper, and last of all, with one soft cloth.

𝒲e know quickly when a conversation is getting valuable: a feeling of new powers developing swiftly, and excitement.

We communicate about what most concerns us. Young people about sex, the old about understanding.

We are married long before ceremonies. We are married before ever we meet.

Wonder why it takes the four-year-old so long, learning to read?
1. Download the Cyrillic alphabet.
2. Start your timer.
3. When you're reading Russian as well as your child's reading English, stop the clock.

When some thoughtful gentle man doesn't dare ask a beautiful woman out, he assumes the lady prefers rich gloss instead of a friend.

When we talk ardently about something we love, and our friends remain silent, then it's safe to know they're not quite so ardent as we.

We see through the eyes of our own experience.

Write 1,000 words a day, writer, every day of your life. Easy for me to say? Sure. And it won't be me cashing your checks.

"She was a beautiful woman, but I met her mind and she changed to dust." It's true, is it? A person's physical beauty changes with the way we think about them?

All I ask of a book is that it engage me in some adventure I've never met before.

Why must we spend years in discomfort before forgiving someone? Why not forgive them now?

Our spouse has an image of us, our parents do, our children do. What matters is our own image of who we are, and why.

When a book is published, the writer taps it softly: "You're on your own, now. Have a good life!" And it's gone.

$\mathcal{A}$ little time, a little perspective, we'll see what the leveling of that site was making room for, in our lives.

$\mathcal{W}$hat makes this world fun is pretending we've forgotten who we are.

*I*t's not a writer's job to sell books. Our book will find its reader if it has to leap screaming from the shelf above (as so many do).

*O*ne of the pleasures of assuming our readers are smart and subtle as foxes, is finding that's most often true.

It's fun to watch how pliable (and sometimes frangible) are the appearances of this world. Every change makes a difference!

Turn our backs on our own happiness to satisfy someone else, and before long we'll be drawing some boundaries.

The secret to a happy lifetime:

1. Find what you love to do, more than anything in all the world.

2. Do it, no matter how difficult it may be.

3. Share the gifts of what your love has taught, with anyone who cares to know.

(1, 2, and 3 are secrets only to those who believe they have to get a job and work to death at what they hate to do.)

We are perfect expressions of perfect Love, here and now.

"*I*'ll just be along for the ride." We've defined our career, as a writer.

*W*e're painters at work on the portrait of our lifetimes. Each choice: one brushstroke.

My suggestion to young people is one simple eternal precept: find what you love and throw yourself toward it with every ounce of your being. At first there will be a thousand barriers and obstacles and dragons in the way -- the dragons are just to test the quality of your love. Press on, and miraculously the way will open up.
You'll blink a few years later and find that everything you dreamed is true around you in daily life. Give the gift of who you are and what you've learned, the world will embrace and support you for doing that.

Our power to choose is limited only by our belief that we don't have the power to choose.

If they didn't mean to hurt me, I'll not feel hurt. If they did mean to hurt me, I'll not feel hurt just for spite.

Self-consciousness kills writers. We must not care what the publisher thinks, what the reader thinks...we must not care what we think, till we've written, "~ end ~."

Learned from a microscope and a drop of pond-water: Shift our focus, see a different world.

$\mathcal{T}$he nice thing about not using profanity is that when we do, it has a powerful effect!

$\mathcal{I}$t is one thing to believe in levitation when you see it, it is another thing entirely to believe in miracles.

*I*ntuitively, we know that we are ageless and the body lifeless. Or better, the body has the same life that an airplane has...it all depends on the pilot's spirit.

*T*he constant among most good secrets involves the giving of something to others, yet the giving of something to ourselves is important, too.

*N*EVER send a manuscript for publication when we do not love, every word!

"*F*iction," "Non-fiction." Doesn't matter. This matters: are our ideas true, will they work in our reader's life?

*F*lying itself is a constant dynamic, in which the flyer must ever think what will happen next: will my velocities keep me safe or drift me toward dangers? To be aloft and not have to think ahead, to suspend time and float, to close the eyes and open them at leisure still floating...there's infinite creative luxury!

*I*t isn't anyone else's power, to make us unhappy. Lucky us: it's ours.

When we don't believe we control our world, we leave it in the hands of those who do.

We're not kind to others in order to meet their needs, but to meet our own. We're kind because we like being kind.

*I*t's not our airline captain who needs to practice flying, it's our student pilot; though giving him the controls can make our ride a bit rough.

*S*uffering: A loss of perspective, a belief that we're helpless and alone and powerless to change the world we perceive.

$\mathcal{A}$ book is a private dialog with its reader, and can be the same for no two readers, even when we're the author.

$\mathcal{L}$ife doesn't give us money. Life gives us ideas, which we may convert into money whenever we wish.

Our higher sense is always there for us to connect with. One quick path is affirmation: one deep breath, relax your body; second breath, relax your mind; third, know that you are at the level you wish to be, in touch with whichever inner person or idea offers the gift you need right now.

I'm open for any idea that suggests that we are unlimited expressions of perfect life, with tips on ways of demonstrating that in daily life. We all know this, and when we ask for details we will be shown them all around us, in events, in books, in the remarks of others.

*D*reams are the night highways of our imagination. Drive with our video-cam ON.

*T*here are no guarantees, yet there are many probabilities.

Selfish: Acting in the interest of what brings us the highest sense of well-being, long term. The more clearly we understand that interest, the more altruistic we'll seem, to others.

$y$ou can't tell authors by their bookshelves, by what they read. Who they are, most of 'em, it's splashed all over everything they write.

Every idea's guided to those who need to find it. How that works, I don't have a clue.

Dream that life is pointless, it is. Dream that it matters, it does.

Of course we hope to win our chess-game. The outcome's determined not by our hope, but by what we've learned on the board, by our ability to adapt to sudden change.

Responsible: Able to respond, able to answer for our actions to whomever needs to know. Ourselves, for instance.

𝓕or every act we do, there are prices we must pay, and for every act there is a consequence, happy for us or unhappy or neutral.

𝓦hen our target's a donut, and we hit it dead center, we miss.

*I*t's still fun to imagine what our future selves would say, and write it down...a private letter to ourselves. Remarkable, what that soul can tell us!

*S*acrifice: Giving up something we value for something we value less. Of what possible use is that?

Our beliefs are not nothing. They are stronger than steel and harder than stone.

Skydiving's a thrill, but after a while we wish we could get the thing to climb.

Can we name one example of objective good? I can't find one in all the world, that another person wouldn't question.

Why long for a past that we have loved? Better long for a future we can love. That, we can bring to be!

*I*t's hard to find exceptional people, that's why it's fun to be one.

*M*ost often we lack answers because we forgot to ask questions.

*T*he right person walks through the turns and labyrinths to the inner us as though we'd built no walls at all.

*I*t is easy to lose sight of the nourishments that made us what we were...music, flight, etc. When these are gone, we go dull unless other nourishments replace it. Don't let go of them until we don't wish to have them and we are ready and wanting new nourishments.

$\mathcal{E}$mpathy overcomes fear and hostility. Name that spider "Cathy," and we probably won't be killing her.

$\mathcal{O}$ur highest obligation to others is to do what we most love to do.

We're mosaics joined in rainbows, yet from time to time it's hard to see the beauty of our own colors. Just wait.

Once we settle our thoughts about dying, when we know that it's a happy graduation and not a fearful error, we can finally get on with true living.

Then we'll see that living is all there is to do.

*M*ost of us know What happens in our lives, but we don't learn How till later and Why till last of all.

*O*ur gifts of love have worked lifetime after lifetime, and they'll work in this lifetime, too!

*I*gnore the call to follow that which we love, and sure enough, our lives get tangled in thorns.

*I*f our favorite writer can open so much in one little chapter, imagine what will happen as she writes more! Basically she's teaching applied empathy, and with those examples to show how well it has worked for her. We'll be excited and try being empathetic ourselves!

*I*t isn't that we don't have time for it, it's that we won't give priority for it.

*T*he image is a dream, and the beauty is real— can you see the difference?

Sometimes I'll get caught in part of a story that looks like it's going nowhere, and it will feel dull to me. That's OK. If it feels dull later, reading it, I'll just cut it out, or rewrite it with style. I do a lot of rewriting. The only thing the reader will see is the final draft, so I just rewrite till I love the final draft. Nobody will know that there used to be an awkward sentence there, or that this paragraph didn't fit smoothly in this place before. It does now, and they will find that pretty neat.

$\mathcal{N}$o book's worth writing, or reading, unless somehow it can touch us.

$\mathcal{T}$he difference between rescuing and helping is the rescuer does all the work.

Sometimes writers need unusual word orders, odd neologisms, strange punctuations. Sometimes we'll need readers to slow here, speed there, and we'll make that happen no matter the rules.

When we think about our prices and think about our priorities, we can be walking wide eyed into our adventures. Of course we can be stumbling blindfolded into whatever may happen, too.

How to Forget a Terrific Idea: "No need to bother with a note. I'll remember this one!"

The whole point of writing is to connect with a few like souls, to join a family of mind.

The Getting-Used-To Syndrome: She was once a kitten abandoned at the roadside. Now she won't eat if her lettuce has the wrong dressing on it.

To a giant redwood, does a hummingbird exist? What other lives, no matter how beautiful, happen so quickly we don't notice?

We all use our own definitions, we are all lexicographers, it is we who elevate and shape the language, not dictionaries and professors.

Our destiny talks with us through small events, passing comments, people we meet by chance. We listen by noticing.

*T*hose who sacrifice their interests for ours, they usually want something in return.

*W*hen we're separated from a love we see it through the barbed-wire of the "reason" for the separation, and the reason itself is invisible. We yearn to be with the love again, and that means travelling back in time, or finding a way to cut our way through the fence. But in our heart we know that this love, past present or future, is not gone.

*A*m I making this up? I make everything up. You're the ones who decide if what I make up works for you.

*T*here's a magnet that's pulling on us, pulling against the fence of this world's limits. We were born on the other side of the fence.

When we hate our work, we don't have time to do what we love. When we love our work, we don't have time to do what we hate.

Every choice we make, brings its consequence into our lives. If we choose the fun of creativity, if we choose to give gifts to others of what we've found along the path of our own adventures, we'll discover a sense of well-being, a happiness that we'll miss when we live to lesser standards.

The river of life knows where it is going. It delights to lift us free of any obstacle, whenever we dare let go.

When we think of our work as a "job," we're in the wrong business.

*I*f we choose not to accept a change in our writing, it's because we've thought about it, and finally decided we're happier with the original.

*E*very book is the best book I knew how to write at the time. The next will be the best book I'll know how to write next. We can go forward, but there's no going back.

$\mathcal{W}$e learn most when we play against an opponent who can beat us.

$\mathcal{W}$e wear human costumes in order to exist in this world, but in no way do we require our costumes in order to survive.

*I*f we want a quick tour through hell, we can stop loving. Hell is a place, a time, a consciousness, in which there is no love. Sex, lust, adventure, excitement -- yes. But not love. How long can we stay in hell?

*A*viation is a calling that cherishes understatement. Set against the backdrop of nature so enormous, so able to swat one tumbling like a leaf, pilots have found that to understate is the only way to hint at the realities they face every day.

$\mathcal{Y}$ou are led through your life by the inner learning creature, the playful spiritual being that is your real self.

$\mathcal{E}$very suggestion for change is a threat to some status quo.

My secret hideaway, oddly enough, is everywhere: it's the sky. Like most folks who fly, there's an instant perspective that comes from lifting away from the ground. It's easy to see the beautiful and the true, when we're flying, and impossible not to bring a bit of that back with us when we land.

Dragons swim in waters that are boring for most of us: evil, destruction, broken cities. We meet dragons only when we choose to travel to the places where they live.

Happiness is the end of our rainbow. It's a million rays of flashing sunlight, vanishing the grey world that once surrounded us.

We bring into our lives that which we hold in our thought.

𝒯ry rejecting "I love," and watch what happens to our sense of well-being. Without some touch of love, it disappears, replaced by an answerless question: "What's it all about?" For what it's all about, is love!

𝒲ant to be a writer? Three tests, just this side of impossible:
Have fun.
Don't think.
Don't care.

$\mathcal{W}$e write our own scripts. We're responsible for the terrible mistakes on our pages, and we're responsible for the delights we've written, too.

$\mathcal{E}$nthusiasm is our telescope: it magnifies what we love and vanishes anything else.

To fly an airplane, we must trust what we cannot see: there are no strings or wires that lift an airplane into the sky.

Yet there is an unseen principle, called aerodynamics, which does lift us. The more we learn of the principle, the more freedom we find, and delight, the more perspective we are given. So it is in living, I think. The more we learn to trust the unseen principle, the more we follow our highest right and that which we most love to do, the more freedom and joy we discover in living. As there are many levels available to the aviator, so are there many levels within ourselves, each offering vistas and lessons and powers unknown to those who live without curiosity or discovery or hope or light, and therefore without joy.

The difficulty about adolescence is that we're not prepared for it until we're 30 or so. By then we've somehow muddled through our 'teens.

We love being surprised by our story itself and do our best writing in a mouth-open-astonished position.

$\mathcal{A}$dvice, as we become writers?

Write a thousand words a day, every day of your life. We'll find that the more we write, the better our writing (that is, the happier our writing makes us feel).

$\mathcal{N}$o matter how good an editor you may be, my way to cut 50 pages from my book will be different from your way. What's seamless for the editor, will be awkward for the writer.

We needn't carry old baggage into new adventures, unless we decide that we need to drag them along wherever we go.

Flying gave me a homeland, the sky. It taught me perspective, gave me ideas that were pleasures to share.

I believe that whatever the calling that we love, we will find in it a metaphor of living itself, parallels that we can call on for our own entertainment and education. A person who loves gardening, for instance, will find in her garden all the same lessons that I find in the sky.

*W*e care more about what happens in our life, than anyone else. We have the power to control it, to move our life in any direction we wish. Learn this, and we've found the key to our own happiness.

Consider our decisions to be as the means to the life in which we choose to live.

We write when we have something to say. Writing is one way of sharing the gifts we've already been given.

The easiest part of writing books has been to give up the ambition, once and for all, that we might become a sophisticated and literary writer.

Our truth may never stop being true for us in the world, but for others it could be lies. We perceive a world of appearances, and through our perception, everything's subjective.

I'm one who often follows the no-problem path. I rarely recognize limitations, no matter they're staring at me through spiral eyes.

*F*lying taught me that fear comes from ignorance, and fear vaporizes with understanding. Discovery lifts us above our frights.

*T*he effect of a piece of writing on the thinking and understanding of others is inversely proportional to its length. Tomes deaden, brilliant writing electrifies.

*R*eaders deserve a story that is first-time new to them, and unexpected. It's after a book is published and popular, that a reader might care to learn how the scenes were done.

$\mathcal{W}$e live in a magical world and we are all of us magicians free to practice our dominion over the worlds of our own beliefs.

$\mathcal{T}$hat we perceive limitations does not make the limitations real, no matter how violent or destructive they may appear.

We ask for forgiveness, not because we need to be forgiven but we need our own peace of mind. With forgiveness, we've done what we can to redress the wrong that was our responsibility. Our balloon can drop these sandbags of guilt and gain altitude!

I write to entertain and to remind myself, knowing that as I do, I will automatically entertain and remind a few others of my own family of values.

$\mathcal{M}$arriage doesn't define a soulmate, nor does divorce dissolve one.

$\mathcal{O}$pportunities sometimes come in strange disguise, tests that let us demonstrate what we know and who we are.

Place is a function of time: "The NY Armory on 32nd and Park Ave" is a place only relative to 1897-1970. The place does not exist as a function of 1980. And time has no meaning without place. If we are on Arcturus 4, or in some totally different galaxy or universe, is there any meaning to "1982"?

Without a desire to do anything, we won't make it happen -- no matter that others think we ought to do.

We learn most about others in the presence of their daily choices, and their ideas.

The gift that writers share is their view of the world and our place in it. As far as I can tell, there's a scenario that follows when we decide to give our gift: first everything conspires to see if it can make us quit. Dragons of all sorts and sizes, disasters sent to crush us. Yet somehow, goes my theory, when we trust and declare in spite of dragons that we will give what we have chosen to give, no matter what, a principle of coincidence moves, things gradually turn around, and we survive. Later, we prosper to the point that others look at us and say, "It was easy, for you..."

What we say tells others nothing. What we do, tells them everything.

One test of an idea is the retrofit protocol: have we been thinking this all along and not noticed?

The most difficult task is to find what it is that we most love to do. This requires self-examination. Doing what we love requires only persistence and dedication.

We don't find independence, we don't find freedom, without major risks. Every awareness comes at a price. I choose to write as I wish, yet the price is that I'll consider the most outlandish consequence of the most innocent choice I may choose.

*L*ocation is immaterial. The landscape that matters for the writer, is found within.

*T*he whole reason for this lifetime is to experience love in a million different ways.

*I*f we don't care to know how far it is to distant planets, even when we understand our math, we still won't care to know how far they are.

*T*he world of space, time and appearances can be wondrous beautiful. Just don't mistake them for real.

$\mathcal{A}$rgue for our limitations, and we're in a real minority among our multidimensional pals.

$\mathcal{E}$ven children are captains of their own boats.

*A*ll else fades before

"I love..."

Please enjoy other products by Kind Heart Productions!

Jonathan Livingston Seagull Interactive Audiobook Part 1

Android:
https://play.google.com/store/apps/details?id=com.kindheartproductions.jls1

iOS:
https://itunes.apple.com/app/id1305707988

Jonathan Livingston Seagull Complete Audiobook

https://www.audible.com/pd/Classics/Jonathan-Livingston-Seagull-The-New-Complete-Edition-Audiobook/B079MF8JPX?asin=B079MF8JPX

R Quotes: Daily quotes from Richard Bach

Android:

https://play.google.com/store/apps/details?id=com.kindheartproductions.rquotes

iOS:

https://itunes.apple.com/app/id1416466429

Made in the USA
Coppell, TX
16 December 2019